HAMISH

His Story

First published by Resonate & Blue in 2015
(Imprint of Tatterdemalion Blue)

Words © Angela & Craig Mair 2015
Photographs/Illustrations © By Kind Permission 2015
Front Cover © eclectech.co.uk

Angela and Craig Mair have asserted their right
to be identified as the authors of this work in accordance with
the Copyright, Design and Patents Act 1988

All rights reserved. No part of this publication may be reproduced,
stored in a retrieval system, or transmitted in any form or by any means,
electronic, mechanical, photocopying, recording or otherwise,
without the prior permission of the copyright owner

A CIP catalogue record for this book is available from the British Library

Cover design and layout by Tatterdemalion Blue

ISBN 978-0-9933114-1-3

Tatterdemalion Blue
8 Upper Bridge Street
Stirling
FK8 1ER

www.tatterdemalionblue.com

HAMISH
His Story

Angela & Craig Mair

CONTENTS

Special Thanks

Acknowledgements

Chapter One .... Hamish's early years

Chapter Two .... Hamish at the Smith

Chapter Three .... The campaign to save Hamish

Chapter Four .... Hamish becomes a star

Chapter Five .... Early years at Kilmahog

Chapter Six .... New friends for Hamish

Chapter Seven .... Hamish in old age

SPECIAL THANKS

This book has been a labour of love, but it could not have been written without the support
of many people who helped with information and photographs of Hamish.
I must especially mention Sion Barrington, Michael McGinnes and Elspeth King
at the Smith, and all the staff at the Trossachs Woollen Mill.

Also, I could not have completed this book without my husband Craig,
who is an experienced writer and historian with the research skills which I don't have,
and who has encouraged me all the way.

Angela Stewart Mair
Stirling, May 2015

ACKNOWLEDGEMENTS

Everyone who assisted me has been listed below in alphabetical order,
and I am truly very grateful to them all.

Angela Stewart Mair
Stirling, May 2015

PEOPLE

Sion Barrington, previous owner of Hamish
Annette Brown, Strathyre
Lorna Casson, Cumbria
Bryan Conlan, Manager, Scottish Wool Centre, Aberfoyle
Peter Innes, past manager, Scottish Wool Centre, Aberfoyle,
now manager Trossachs Woollen Mill, Kilmahog
Donald Finlayson, the Hairy Coo bus company
David Grinly, Alva
Elspeth King, curator, the Smith Art Gallery and Museum, Stirling
Michael McGinnes, Hamish's personal carer, the Smith Art Gallery and Museum, Stirling
Marion McIntyre, past owner of the Trossachs Inn, Gartmore Station
Danny McKirgin, Callander Round Table
Steven McLaren, Trossachs Woollen Mill, Kilmahog
John Moffat, Hamish's personal carer, Trossachs Woollen Mill, Kilmahog
Pam McNicol, Stirling Council Archivist
Jim Mailer, Whyler Photos, Stirling
Claire Muir, previous manageress Trossachs Woollen Mill, Kilmahog
Murray O'Donnell, Strathblane Heritage Society
Ian Rodger BVMS MRCVS, Forth Valley Vets, Stirling
Amy Wiseman, Timberbush Tours, Edinburgh

IMAGES

Caledonian Marts Ltd, Stirling
eclectech.co.uk
Peter Doe, Edinburgh
David Kerr Gray
Marion McIntyre
Steven McLaren, Trossachs Woollen Mill, Callander
Craig Mair
George Mair
Graeme Mair
Brandy Sinisi, Farmington, Connecticut, USA
Sion Barrington
Stirling Observer
Smith Art Gallery and Museum, Stirling
Timberbush Tours, Edinburgh
Trossachs Woollen Mill, Callander
Whyler Photos, Stirling
Jeremy Wyatt, Dunblane

Hamish (eclectech.co.uk)

HAMISH

Chapter One

Hamish (Stirling Smith Art Gallery and Museum)

Hamish's early years

I first met Hamish when he was just three years old and I was in my early forties. I was going through a very difficult time in my own life and this lovely piece of highland beefcake was the perfect distraction. For almost twenty years we kept in touch, meeting regularly and learning about each other until his death near the Scottish town of Callander in November 2014. Like millions of other people all across the world, I was broken-hearted. But I was especially broken-hearted, for twenty years earlier I had helped to save his life.

    The story of Hamish is unique. By a string of extraordinary chance events this wonderful animal became the most famous Highland bull in the world. After a very long and happy life Hamish died peacefully in his native Scotland, but by that time this gentle giant, famed for his amazing love of people and a great appetite for turnip, carrots, potatoes and apples, was perhaps more photographed than Scottish actor Sean Connery, probably as celebrated as Scotland's national poet Robert Burns, and definitely as loved as any teddy bear in the land. He really had become a legend in his own lifetime.

    His story is unique because nowadays, in this world of intensive farm production and great concerns for animal welfare, very few Highland male cattle live beyond two or three years - Hamish lived to the ripe old age of 21. This book is my account of how that happened. It is a story worth telling.

    Highland cattle are one of Scotland's great attractions, much photographed by tourists from all over the world. Their brown shaggy coats and enormous horns set cameras clicking wherever they are found. They seem to have a special way of standing in the most photogenic places - almost intentionally posing in the most scenic glens, or knee-deep in the waters of the most beautiful lochs in Scotland. They have become iconic symbols of Scotland, and none more so than Hamish.

HAMISH His Story

Unlike many other cattle breeds, Highland cattle are native to Scotland. They have been around since at least the sixth century, and are said to be the oldest pedigree breed in the world. Originally there were two types of 'Kyloe' - the smaller black coated type of the west coast and the western islands, and the larger red coated cattle from the Highlands. With their thick shaggy coats they could survive Scotland's cold, wet and often snowy winters without having to be brought indoors, so they were a basic part of any highland farmer's stock.

When farming improvements began in the 18th century, clan chiefs and highland families began to take a greater pride in their cattle, competing with each other to produce and own the finest beasts. They became especially popular because, as well as looking great, they were very hardy and sturdy to look at but very gentle in nature. A Highland Cattle Society was formed in 1884 and gradually a wider variety of colours was bred into the Highland herds, including red, black, yellow, dun, white, brindle and silver. Highland cattle were much prized by their owners - they still are, as a visit to any agricultural show in Scotland will quickly prove.

But this is only one side of the story. Farmers don't keep cattle just to draw the tourists. Highland bulls are bred and, at the age of two or three, are then killed, for their excellent meat.

Normally they are castrated when still very young (and so become bullocks rather than bulls), and are then fed well to become fine big animals ready for the butcher's knife. Marketing people like to use the iconic image of Scotland's Highland cattle when selling Scotland's wonderful meat produce to the world.

So this is the first example of the good luck which Hamish would enjoy throughout his life - fate smiled on him, and he survived that dangerous time in his early years, when he might easily have been sent to the slaughter-house for his beef.

However, enough of the background. Let's get on to the life story of the most famous Highland bull in the world.

Hamish's early years

Alyth Agricultural Show 2006. (Craig Mair)

Braco Agricultural Show 2009. (Craig Mair)

Hamish's early years

Our wonderful Hamish was born on 8th February 1993 on the Auchencraig estate farm, owned by Colonel M P de Klee, on the island of Mull. Hamish's father was a bull called Joseph of Cladach, and his ear tag number (which stayed with him for life) was Klee23. Colonel de Klee's intention was to raise Hamish as a bullock for beef production and sell him on again at a market further south to someone with a herd, to be fattened up for slaughter and the butcher's shop.

Mull is one of the most beautiful islands on the west coast of Scotland, just a ferry ride away from the bustling port of Oban. Hamish spent his first three years on this island, carefree and happy in a place with fresh air and good grass, until he was old enough to be separated from his mother and sent south to market.

As it happened, that market was in Stirling where, at the age of just three years, but already growing into a magnificent Highland bullock, Hamish would become famous.

Meanwhile, in 1996 the Smith Art Gallery and Museum in Stirling had decided to hold an exhibition of the works of Joseph Denovan Adam (1841-1896). He was a famous Scottish landscape artist and especially a painter of Highland cattle. At that time the Smith Art Gallery and Museum possessed five of his wonderful paintings, but they were able to negotiate the loan of another 50 and so hold a special show to celebrate the work of this artist.

Although born in Glasgow, Denovan Adam grew up in London where you might think there would be nothing to stir any interest in Highland cattle. His father was a landscape artist and did much to persuade the young man to train at the Royal College of Art and later at the Royal Academy, and to submit paintings for London exhibitions.

However, his parents also took him on sketching holidays to Scotland where he came to admire the scenery and the animal life, such as Scotland's distinctive Clydesdale horses, the blackface sheep and Highland cattle, which he found there. These were so different from anything to be seen in London. Encouraged by these Scottish holidays, the young Denovan Adam began to visit London cattle markets, to understand better the bone structure of animals, and so to draw them better. This interest seems to have spurred him to return to Scotland permanently at the age of 30. He lived in various locations and had two daughters by his first wife, who died soon after. He later remarried, however, and in 1887 moved in to a house at Craigmill, a hamlet on the outskirts of Stirling on the Alloa Road (and which is still there today).

Across the road from his house he had a paddock with a glass studio in the middle of the field, surrounded by animal enclosures for horses and foals, sheep and lambs, goats and hens, but especially for Highland cattle. This glass building allowed Adam, and the many

'Cattle', by Joseph Denovan Adam. (Stirling Smith Art Gallery and Museum)

'Going to Pasture', by Joseph Denovan Adam. (Stirling Smith Art Gallery and Museum)

students who came each year to learn from him, to sit indoors and study these animals in all weathers and from every angle. This helped him to portray them very accurately when he later came to paint them into his highland landscape scenes.

The great artist Sir Edwin Landseer, perhaps the most popular painter of romantic Scottish highland landscapes in Victorian times, is reported to have said that 'there have only been two great creators of landscapes - God, and Denovan Adam'.

Denovan Adam's small herd of Highland cattle was especially a great attraction in Stirling. These magnificent animals were not often seen by local people in Victorian times,

The sale ring at the Caledonian Mart as it looked in the early 2000's. This is where Sion Barrington bought Hamish. (Caledonian Marts Ltd)

being still generally bred only in the highlands of Scotland and rarely seen further south. Like Hamish later, they were a great attraction in their day.

To mark the centenary of Denovan Adam's death, the Smith Art Gallery and Museum decided to hold a 4-month exhibition of his paintings, especially since so many of his works had been created at his local Stirling studio. The 'Smith' is a handsome sandstone building on Dumbarton Road, founded in 1874 by the artist Thomas Smith. It is a fine Victorian building, with Greek-style columns at the front, and surrounded by spacious garden grounds. It was an ideal place to display the work of this Victorian artist.

The Smith's art historian Maria Devaney and curator Elspeth King thought that it would be a good idea to promote the exhibition by creating the attraction of a menagerie of some of Denovan Adam's favourite animals. It would be housed on open grassy ground which lay to the left side of the art gallery building, and which could easily be fenced off to keep the animals secure. The novelty and originality of having animals at an art exhibition would surely bring in the crowds, they thought.

Hamish with Sion Barrington outside the Smith Art Gallery and Museum in Stirling, at the opening of the Joseph Denovan Adam exhibition on 27th April 1996. (Sion Barrington)

Elspeth went for help to Sion Barrington, a well-known shepherd from the hills around Loch Katrine in the beautiful Trossachs part of Scotland. At that time Sion (pronounced like Shaun) had the largest flock of sheep in Britain and lived on the shores of the loch at Glengyle House, once the home of the famous Scottish outlaw Rob Roy. He agreed to help, and so sheep and goats were acquired - that was a start. But what they really needed were some Highland cattle.

Hamish with Sion Barrington outside the Smith Art Gallery and Museum in Stirling, at the opening of the Joseph Denovan Adam exhibition on 27th April 1996. (Sion Barrington)

Hamish's early years

Hamish and some of his friends at the Smith. (Stirling Smith Art Gallery and Museum)

Maria and curator Elspeth wanted a female Highland cow and a calf, which they felt would have a cute appeal to exhibition visitors. But Sion advised that this would be a big mistake! Female cattle come into season approximately every three weeks - did the Smith really want their neighbours to have a cow in heat, moo-ing as loudly as she could for a mate, keeping them awake at night and driving everyone within hearing distance crazy? Perhaps not!

Instead, Sion said that he would find a young Highland male, but one which looked a bit feminine! He explained that the horns of female Highland cows grow pointing upwards, whereas those of castrated male bullocks develop pointing more downwards. So Sion went off to the Caledonian Mart, one of the two local cattle auction markets in Stirling, to find a Highland bullock with horns which did not point down too much. Here he met Hamish, brought south to market from the island of Mull and that day up for sale.

In the end Sion bought five bullocks, but Hamish had the most feminine look and, with another smaller bullock called Hector, was selected for duty as part of the Smith's animal collection. Who would have thought it - Hamish, who would later become the most famous piece of Highland beefcake in the world, only did so because, when he was young, he looked so feminine!

And so it was that in April 1996 Hamish, and what was billed as his 'little brother' Hector, arrived from Mull to become the star attractions at an art exhibition in Stirling. Little did anyone know what lay ahead!

The paddock at the Smith with all the animals. (Stirling Smith Art Gallery and Museum)

HAMISH

Chapter Two

Hamish, with Hector behind him, in the paddock at the Smith.
(Stirling Smith Art Gallery and Museum)

Hamish at the Smith

Hamish was an immediate hit at the Smith Art Gallery and Museum in Stirling. Everyone loved the impressive big hairy 'coo'. He was usually called a cow (which is female) by visitors, although he was really a bullock! Fortunately he didn't seem to mind, and simply got on with meeting people and posing for photos.

Hamish with Sion Barrington outside the Smith. (Stirling Smith Art Gallery and Museum)

HAMISH His Story

Children especially loved to come and see Hamish and his friends. Little brother Hector was actually quite shy, but there were also three lively goats, Magnus the Shetland ram, and several other breeds of sheep including an Australian merino called Ballerina Pete ... no one knows why he was called this name! But Hamish was the star of the show - a great favourite of the visitors because he was so gentle and tame by cattle standards. As with many animals he just seemed to know the amount he would tolerate and with whom.

This made him particularly suited for meeting children and people with special needs. The hands-on experience of patting and stroking, and especially of combing Hamish's lovely brown hair, helped give them an interest and a sense of achievement and fun.

Hamish was always wonderful with children. (Sion Barrington)

Hector gets a tit-bit to eat. (Sion Barrington)

The Herald newspaper summed up Hamish's popularity in an article by Aileen Little in July 1996, when it said: "It has to be said, Elspeth King doesn't make a habit of throwing herself at members of the opposite sex: as curator of the Smith Art Gallery and Museum in Stirling, she is normally a model of propriety. But Hamish is special. He is drop dead gorgeous … Hamish is a bull for all seasons, a natural star. "He's a stunning animal, just beautiful. We have come to love him," enthuses King, clearly smitten. "Maintaining the condition of Hamish's russet locks is a task the Smith's team vie for - along with attending to his dietary needs. People travel from far and wide to pay homage to Hamish and to paint him (art classes are part of the 1996 programme) …"

Sion and Hamish do a presentation at one of the Smith's plant sale days. (Sion Barrington)

Even the neigbours didn't mind the crowds or the noise. According to museum curator Elspeth King, recalling those days when interviewed in 2014, "The neighbours were wonderfully supportive, and Colonel and Mrs Saunders of Royal Gardens, who enjoyed waking up to the lowing of cattle in the morning, kept an eye out for them."

One unforeseen bonus was the generous amount of dung which Hamish and his companions produced during the summer. This was sold for manure to enthusiastic gardeners at the Smith's annual sale of plants - Stirling's gardens never looked so luxuriously green as they did during that summer of 1996!

David Brown of the Friends of the Smith organisation recalled later: "In 1996 the Plant Sale was again one of my main concerns, and during July, August and September, the Denovan Adam exhibition's success was supplemented by the presence of Highland cows and rare breeds of sheep and goats in what is now Ailie's Garden. I got much pleasure from assisting with the care of the animals - 'mucking out', feeding and grooming, particularly Hamish ... and teaching the goats to dance during evening feed time."

Hamish listens while the Stirling District Schools Pipe Band play. (Sion Barrington)

At about this time the noted Scottish artist Greer Ralston was engaged by the Smith to make a painting of Hamish. In 2014 she recalled to the Daily Record newspaper: "I was delighted to be commissioned many years ago to paint the portrait of Hamish. Having had a

Greer Ralston's painting of Hamish at the Smith. This image later appeared on the front cover of the national Museums Journal. (Stirling Smith Art Gallery and Museum)

country background and a great love of animals I knew how important and valued Hamish was by Elspeth King and all her team at the Smith". The Smith still holds this painting, and it is also included on the BBC's 'Your paintings' website of paintings on public display in Britain.

In August Hamish made the news when he accidentally became an archaeologist. In the grassy pen where he lived beside the Smith, he unearthed a rare Victorian clay pipe with his hoof. "It's a lovely pipe with a ship on one side and an anchor on the other", said the museum's curator Elspeth King. "I think we'll give him a job as an archaeologist," she added. "After all, I've got the evidence here! Perhaps we could even have him made a Fellow of the Society of Antiquaries of Scotland," she joked.

Unfortunately those happy days were actually no joking matter. Hamish's life at the Smith was in the middle of going disastrously wrong. During the 1990s the dreadful animal disease BSE (bovine spongiform encephalopathy), commonly known as 'mad cow disease', had begun to spread across Britain. This horrible condition caused a spongy degeneration in the brain and spinal cord of cattle which usually killed them.

By 1993 there had been 100,000 cases in Britain. Then in 1995 a new, even more terrifying, disease known as 'new variant CJD' appeared. This seemed to link BSE with the human equivalent, Creutzfeldt–Jakob disease (CJD), and later that year humans began to die from this variant. They caught this disease by eating beef products from cattle infected with BSE.

In March 1996 the European Union announced a worldwide export ban on all British beef. In June the European Union demanded that there should be a selective slaughter programme of 'at risk' animals to speed up the eradication of BSE in Britain. Most of these cattle were young animals because they were most likely to be incubating the disease, so an 'over 30 month' slaughter scheme was started. The intention was that every calf over 30 months would be killed to stop its meat from somehow entering the food chain. In the end over 4 million British cattle were killed, many from herds which had never had BSE before.

As one German blogger posted later: "It was the worst time of the BSE crisis in Great Britain. Pretty much every British cow over 3 years old faced the prospect of slaughter! Period! No exceptions!"

It was a terrible time. People saw huge piles of dead cattle being burned on TV news programmes. Many people stopped buying beef and veal, because they were afraid of catching 'new variant CJD'. It was a kind of hysteria.

Then it was announced that Hamish, who was three years old, would have to be killed as part of the European Union's slaughter programme. He would be allowed to stay at the Smith until the art exhibition ended in early September, but then he would be taken off to the slaughter house.

At about this time the artist George Wyllie did a wire sculpture of the Hamish for a 'name the sculpture' competition, which he called "BSE - Bloody Sorry Everyone". It won the competition, but the chances of Hamish winning a reprieve from the slaughter house seemed low.

I decided to start a campaign to save Hamish from this dreadful fate.

HAMISH

Chapter Three

Hamish, complete with a tartan sash tied round his horns, poses for photos at the opening of the Callander World Highland Games in July 1996. (Sion Barrington)

The campaign to save Hamish

I came to be involved with Hamish in a strange way. Being from a farming family I went to see the wonderful exhibition of Denovan Adam's paintings of Highland cattle at the Smith. Here, like so many other people, I realised what a star attraction Hamish was with locals and visitors alike. You don't see too many buff brown handsome Scottish Highlanders like Hamish at museums! At that time, the Smith was the place to be, and to be seen, and all thanks to an outstanding art exhibition and a few hairy or woolly beauties.

At that time I was working on a Media course run by the Central FM radio station in Stirling. Here I was assigned the project of covering the story behind the sudden appearance of all these farm animals at the Smith. My first port of call was Maria Devaney, the Smith's specialist art historian, and we immediately got on very well with each other, partly through a shared love of the animals now living beside the Gallery. But Hamish, so calm and gentle, quickly proved to be a special sweetheart.

Then, in early July, I learned that Hamish and friends were going to be slaughtered because of the outbreak of BSE. Maria and I wanted to do something to stop this, and I suggested a 'Save Hamish' campaign through the newspapers and radio station. The people at the Smith, perhaps persuaded by Maria, went along with the idea, so I ran it past my boss at Central FM and got the go-ahead.

With help from Tadek Kopszywa, a newsreader at Central FM, I prepared press releases and sent them to every newspaper, news agency and TV station we could think of. Maria and I also took a petition onto the streets of Stirling and began to gather signatures - eventually we ended up with thousands of petition supporters from all over the Stirling area, and many from further away. Soon the 'Save Hamish' campaign was in the news all over Scotland.

We also tried to contact Scottish celebrities to enlist their support. We especially got great help from local Stirling County rugby star Kevin MacKenzie. At that time he was a well-known regular in the Scottish international team, and so our local beefcake rugby star joined the campaign and ended up posing in photos with Hamish. As a man who knew well about hard work and dedication, Kevin was just wonderful in helping us - and of course he came to love Hamish too!

I did a live appeal every week in Central FM's 'Community What's On' programme. I wrote a script (which I still have) and found myself appealing directly to local people to help Save Hamish. I had never spoken on radio before, and to do it as a real presenter was daunting!

Meanwhile the Stirling Observer newspaper gave us great publicity and support. On 17th July 1996 one article said: "A campaign to save a popular Highland bullock from the chop is gathering support throughout the district. Three year old Hamish, who is a star attraction at an exhibition of animal art at the Smith Art Gallery and Museum is earmarked for the slaughterhouse under the regulations of the EU-sponsored cull brought into force to ease the BSE scare.

However, a petition has been organised by animal lover Angela Stewart to help save Hamish and has also enlisted support from people such as Stirling County and Scotland rugby star Kevin McKenzie and from local radio station Central FM.

Angela said: "We want as many people as possible to protest at the senseless killing of an animal who's clearly proved himself to be an asset to the town. He has already had a therapeutic effect. A lot of disabled kids have visited him and had a lot of fun brushing and feeding him."

The educational benefits of having Hamish around should not be overlooked. He teaches youngsters about animal welfare and they learn a bit about how to look after their own pets. After all, Hamish is just a big pet himself."

By now the phone at Central FM was constantly ringing with concerned people calling

Scottish international rugby star Kevin McKenzie poses with Hamish for the newspapers, to help publicise the 'Save Hamish' campaign. (Whyler Photos, Stirling)

about Hamish. Money began to pour in, and we handed this to the Smith where its own campaign, led by the Friends of the Smith, was also getting under way.

At about this time, in mid-July 1996, we had a call from the Round Table organisation in Callander. They wanted to help publicise our campaign, but also to advertise the Callander World Highland Games which they organised each year, and which were to be held in a few days' time. The Callander games especially featured 'strong man' events, including one of the qualifying rounds for the European Strongest Man competition, so they sent some of their big strong competitors along to the Smith to be photographed with Hamish.

Although they were well warned about Hamish's horns, the two big beefy guys climbed into the paddock with our bullock - who posed for a photograph with them, but then immediately sent them sprawling to the ground with one quick shake of his head! After that, these two strong men, contenders for the European Strongest Man competition, refused to go back into the paddock with Hamish! But it was all good fun for the onlookers, and great for the newspapers.

A few days later Hamish left the Smith to be Chieftain of the Callander World Highland Games, which lasted two days. Among his duties that weekend, he led the parade of bagpipers and athletes round the games arena, and posed with visitors for photos in the middle of the park. The insurance people demanded that there should be a special pen with a double fence for Hamish - according to Sion Barrington they provided the required enclosure, but since the insurance company had forgotten to specify that Hamish must be inside it, they left him free to meet people outside it!

Of course, in spite of the insurers' worries, there was never any danger to the public from Hamish. Sion remembers one moment in particular. He recalls a little girl who was posing for a photo in front of Hamish. She started to step further back from the camera and was in danger of bumping backwards into Hamish's horns. Hamish could see what was happening, but the bullock also knew that he could not move out of the way because of people crowding behind him too. Sion says that it was very clear that Hamish realised the problem, so he carefully moved his head so that the little girl was not harmed by his horns when she ended up backing into him.

There was also a 'guess-the-weight-of-Hamish' competition, which raised £160 for the local Strathcarron Hospice. Those two lovely sunny days at Callander, when a bullock was the Chieftain at the games, are still remembered well by many local people.

Back in Stirling our campaign to Save Hamish was now moving quickly. We were receiving calls from lots of national newspapers. One ran a story with a headline which said,

The campaign to save Hamish

Strong men from the Callander World Highland Games pose for a press photo with Hamish. (Whyler Photos, Stirling)

Bull may be saved by the Queen, and suggested that Hamish might join Her Majesty's herds at Balmoral Castle. Offers to give Hamish a home came in from other places too, but my feeling was that these were all too far away.

On 24th July the Stirling Observer wrote another piece about the campaign, under the headline, **Moo-ving response for Hamish the bullock**: "Observer readers have taken the bull by the horns in a bid to save Hamish the bullock from the slaughterhouse ... Angela Stewart, who is spearheading the campaign to save the star attraction of a current exhibition at the

Hamish with some young admirers at the Callander World Highland Games. (Sion Barrington)

The campaign to save Hamish

For some kids, Hamish was very big indeed! (Sion Barrington)

Smith Art Gallery and Museum said: "We have had an offer from Comrie in Perthshire and one from Aberdeenshire, but we are keen for Hamish to stay in the Stirling area. There are two local offers on the table and they offer the animal a permanent place to stay, but we need to raise the £500 to buy him and we are appealing for sponsors to come forward.""

Maria Devaney from the Smith said: "Owner Sion Barrington will not be making a decision about Hamish's future until the exhibition ends at the end of August. We do want him to stay in the area as he has become a pet and it is good for schools and special needs children to visit him. However, Sion is going to have to sell him to the most appropriate place, whether that is in the Stirling area or not."

Sion Barrington said: "I am not in a position to give Hamish away, which would make no sense to me whatsoever. I could get at least 85p per kilo minimum if he was culled in line with the government scheme in light of the BSE scare, but I would rather that did not happen. The over-riding priority is the best career move for him, where his talents for providing educational aspects for school children and therapy for special needs kids can be fully utilised."

By now we were receiving help from others on Central FM's Media course. Five or six of them went out into Stirling's streets with tape recorders to get 'vox pops' - sound-bite recordings of people's reactions to the Hamish campaign, which we then used in Central FM's broadcasts.

Michael McGinnes at the Smith also created a fun biography of Hamish. They called him Hamish McKye Denovan - Kye is a Scottish word for cattle, and McKye made it sound even more Scottish, while Denovan paid tribute to the Victorian artist whose exhibition of paintings Hamish had helped to publicise. He kept this name throughout the rest of his life. According to this biography he was also born on Mull 'under a wandering star', his star sign was Taurus, he had been educated at the University of 'Highland' Life, his horns were 84 cm wide, and so on. It was an excellent piece of publicity.

On 8th August Maria Devaney organised a free illustrated talk on Highland cattle at the Smith. It was given by Angus McKay, past president of the Highland Cattle Society. The campaign was growing.

In mid-August the local schools resumed classes after the summer holidays. Soon they began to get involved in the campaign. The Allan's Primary School and the Bright Beginnings Nursery in Stirling both contacted the Smith with a view to adopting Hamish as a pet.

Meanwhile the decision day on Hamish's future was approaching fast. When asked about this by the Herald newspaper, the Smith's curator Elspeth King was clearly upset. By now Hamish had become such a favourite, she would happily have taken care of him herself -

The campaign to save Hamish

Hamish poses in late July at the Callander Highland Games with Michael Forsyth, the local Conservative MP. At that time, before the opening of Scotland's devolved parliament, he was the Secretary of State for Scotland, so given the hysteria over cattle at the time, it probably helped the 'Save Hamish' campaign to have such a prominent MP willing to stand so close to Hamish! (Marion McIntyre)

but she lived in a flat! Or as she put it to reporter Aileen Little, "A Glasgow tenement doesn't have much room for a Highland cow."

In the end it was Hamish's clear place as a popular pet which saved him. With schools wanting to adopt him, local children coming to visit him at the Smith, special needs kids especially finding him a wonderful experience, and the public signing petitions and donating money to save him from the slaughterhouse, it was very clear that he was a great local pet. To the animal health officials it was quite obvious that Hamish was so loved by the people of Stirling that he would never be in danger of being sent to a butcher's or somehow getting into the local food chain. He was not a BSE or new-variant CJD disease risk to humans.

And so, at the last minute, Hamish's life was spared. We had saved him.

Hamish had a great appetite for turnip, carrots, potatoes and apples.
(Timberbush Tours)

HAMISH

Chapter Four

Hamish and Sion arrive to meet children at a farm life centre in 1997.
(Sion Barrington)

Hamish becomes a star

Now that Hamish was safe, the next thing was to decide his future, and that of the other animals at the Smith. As a first step, their owner Sion Barrington rented Back Borland Farm at Gartmore near the town of Aberfoyle, and arranged to have all the animals moved there when the Smith's art exhibition closed at the beginning of September 1996.

At about that time the Smith, which had benefitted so much from the wonderful publicity generated by Hamish and the other animals, came up with an ingenious suggestion. They wanted to maintain a connection to the bullock which had become so much a part of the art gallery, so the Smith management appointed him as their External Relations Officer! It seems that the intention was that, whenever possible, Hamish would return to his paddock at the museum and undertake publicity appearances in the town. The Smith must surely be the only art gallery in world which has ever had a Highland bull in its top public relations job!

On 4th September the Stirling Observer carried an article with a headline which said simply, **Hamish Saved**.

"The fate of Hamish the highland bullock has finally been decided after weeks of uncertainty. The famous beast will become chief publicity officer of the Smith Art Gallery and Museum, thanks to an appeal organised by the Friends of the Smith which raised nearly £600, more than enough to buy him from owner Sion Barrington.

It is expected that Hamish will use the Smith as his home base, where he will return after engagements. His first port of call will be the Farmlife Centre at Thornhill, followed by a visit to Aberfoyle at Christmas. David Brown, Chairman of the Friends, said: "It has been a great effort by everybody involved. The campaign has also highlighted the museum and attendance figures are up.""

According to Sion Barrington, he did not sell Hamish to the Smith. He feels that the Smith were really the 'moral' owners of Hamish, even if he still retained the bullock's registration papers. However, the Smith did not have the financial resources to provide all the facilities needed on site for keeping Hamish with them permanently, or even just to look after him, to pay for his transportation, maintain his paperwork, and so on. So Sion Barrington and Elspeth King came to an agreement whereby the Friends of the Smith paid a regular small sum to Sion towards Hamish's costs at Back Borland Farm, and in return were able to borrow him for events in Stirling.

And so, on Sunday 15th September 1996, a farewell party was held at the art gallery and, to music from the Central Region Schools Pipe Band, Hamish and the other animals went off with Sion to begin their new life at Back Borland Farm.

Soon after, Hamish's 'little brother' Hector was sent to live in gentle retirement in the grounds of the Ardanaiseig Hotel on the shores of Loch Awe in the highlands. Hamish's future, however, was very different! From then on, his life became a succession of public engagements. He seemed to love it! As External Relations Officer for the Smith, he began to attend all kinds of interesting events. Over the next few years he met royalty, politicians and celebrities, appeared in TV adverts (and in an episode of the popular TV police detective programme 'Taggart'), attended a garden festival, visited local farm life centres, was a guest at numerous gatherings and occasions, and continued to attract a wider and wider circle of admirers.

As Christmas 1996 approached, Hamish made a special appearance at the famous Scottish Wool Centre at Aberfoyle. For the previous few years Sion Barrington had helped provide sheep for a 'Welcome Santa' street parade through the town, but in 1996 he brought Hamish. With crowds lining the main street, Hamish led the Callander Pipe Band and a procession of locals in fancy dress to the Wool Centre as part of the pre-Christmas attractions. He was a sensation.

On another occasion Hamish was a guest at the Trossachs Inn, a pub (now gone) which

Hamish becomes a star

The wooden collection box at the Smith. It's still there today, still collecting money for the art gallery. (Stirling Smith Art Gallery and Museum)

stood at Gartmore Station between the village of Gartmore and the town of Aberfoyle, and not far from Sion Barrington's farm at Back Borland. The landlord then was Alan McIntyre and his widow Marion can still remember the fun and games they had with Hamish, simply trying to turn his head and horns so that he could get through the door. Inside, the floor of the pub was of old flagstones but Hamish behaved himself and there were no accidents!

Meanwhile Hamish also kept in touch with the Smith Art Gallery and Museum. As the Herald newspaper reported in July 1997: "To remind visitors of his special relationship and to raise money for his keep, [the Smith] has obtained a wooden effigy of its Highland bull. The sculpture was made by Liverpudlian artist Frank Egerton with a coin slot and collecting box - and the wooden Hamish rewards each donor by rolling his eyes and flashing a fine set

Sion leads Hamish out of the side door of the Trossachs Inn, where there was ramped access for wheelchairs - and bullocks! (Marion McIntyre)

of teeth, complete with gold filling. Since his arrival we are told Hamish has been coining it in, and gallery boss Elspeth King claims: "It's probably the first time a wooden cow has been milked so well!""

In September 1997 Hamish returned to the Smith to stay there for a time. David Brown of the Friends of the Smith organisation wrote later online that "when Hamish returned in September 1997 I was his full-time carer; the grass was waist-high and he couldn't eat it, nor could I find his droppings! So with a borrowed scythe I set to, to create a usable paddock and a reserve of fresh straw for his comfort and consumption".

On 7th May 1998 Hamish made a special guest appearance at the Marches shopping centre in Stirling. This extension to the Thistles Centre had been opened back in September

1997 but the celebrations had been curtailed by the tragic death of Princess Diana - her funeral was the day after the Marches were opened. So in May 1998 a bigger fun day was organised, and of course Hamish was there! Indeed, he even made a grand entrance by arriving in the lift from the car park!

LOAD OF BULL: Hamish and "Keeper" Sion Barrington are prevented from entering the china shop in the Marches

HOLD ON THERE HAMISH!

May 1998, outside Whittard's china shop in the Marches shopping centre in Stirling.
Sion Barrington pleads with police to be allowed to take Hamish into the shop. (Stirling Observer)

One highlight of the day was when Sion Barrington spotted Whittard's tea and china shop (which was at Unit 10 of the Marches in those days). He could not resist the temptation to take his bull into this china shop. Of course Hamish behaved impeccably and nothing was broken, but according to Sion, when they re-emerged from the shop into the concourse outside, they were met by two rather concerned police officers. Someone persuaded them to pose for a photo, which later appeared in the Stirling Observer. It shows Sion pleading with the police officers to be allowed to take his bull into the shop, but according to Sion it was a spoof and the 'bull in a china shop' incident really did happen, and remains one of his favourite memories of Hamish.

Another highlight of that day was when Hamish decided to relieve himself in the concourse area. Sion could see the warning signs and quickly informed a couple of cleaners nearby of the impending mess, but they were on their tea break and decided not to mop up until they were finished. And so it was Sion who had to advise nearby shoppers to stand well back while Hamish did his business - he must surely be the only farm animal ever to have done the toilet in the middle of the Marches shopping area in Stirling.

Such events helped spread Hamish's name well beyond the Stirling area. Shortly after his adventures in the shopping centre Hamish even starred in a cartoon in the Beano comic! This was produced and published at Dundee, about 60 miles away, but was read by hundreds of thousands of children all over Britain.

During 1999 Hamish was sometimes back at the Smith Art Gallery and Museum, as on 19th November when he made a special appearance, and again in May 2000 when he was there to help promote the annual plant sale.

In September 1999 Hamish and Sion went to help promote the image of Scottish beef at a Farmers' Market being held at the famous Glasgow Barrowlands open-air market (often called simply 'the Barras'). When they arrived they were greeted by a very large and fierce-looking dog. The locals obviously thought that their dog would frighten Hamish, but Sion

A still from a security camera at the Marches captures Hamish in the concourse, arousing the curiosity of the public. (Sion Barrington)

laughed and said simply, "my money's on the bull!". Of course, in the end all went well at the Barras and Hamish was a big draw for crowds to the farmers' market.

After their appearance there Sion and Hamish were invited in for refreshment by the landlord of a nearby pub. This place had swing doors and Sion still remembers that, as they pushed through, one of the three old men who were sitting inside simply looked round and said, "Oh, there's a hielan' coo just come in" - and with that they went on with the more important business of their drinking!

Hamish and Sion arrive to meet children at a farm life centre in 1997. (Sion Barrington)

On 24th March 2000 Hamish was the special guest at a highland games event held at Duntreath Castle near Blanefield. Having been the star of these games he then went on to spend the rest of that day as a special public relations attraction at the nearby Glengoyne distillery, where he was greatly admired by a Russian delegation that was being shown round.

Over the years Hamish also made several more appearances at the famous Scottish Wool Centre at Aberfoyle, including a pre-Christmas visit in November 2000. In 2001 he was the main Christmas attraction at the woollen centre, being resident there from 23rd November to 24th December.

Hamish becomes a star

In 2002 the Scottish Wool Centre's assistant manageress Linda Hannah moved to become the manageress at the Trossachs Woollen Mill at Kilmahog, just outside Callander. She had seen at Aberfoyle what an attraction Hamish could be, and so, with approval from her bosses at the Edinburgh Woollen Mill company, she negotiated during that year with Sion Barrington and the Smith Art Gallery and Museum to bring Hamish to Kilmahog.

Hamish munching daffodils outside the Smith. (Sion Barrington)

It was seen at the time as a kind of 'retirement' for Hamish - a rest from all the personal appearances he had recently been making. At the time it is probably fair to say that no-one could have foreseen the extraordinary future which Hamish would now go on to enjoy. It proved to be anything but a quiet retirement!

Not long after, Sion Barrington passed Hamish's official registration documents on to Linda Hannah at the Trossachs Woollen Mill. While the Smith still retained some say over their bullock's future, the gallery was always tight for funding, even for its own day-to-day expenses, and did not really have the resources to support Hamish too. In reality, practical decisions about Hamish now lay with the staff at Kilmahog who now held his registration documents, and to some extent with their owners, the Edinburgh Woollen Mill company. While it must have been hard for the Smith staff to see the publicity and income which Hamish now brought to Callander, in general this arrangement worked well.

With this move to Kilmahog, a whole new chapter in Hamish's life was about to begin - one which would spread his name far beyond Scotland and win him friends and fans across the world.

Hamish at the Trossachs Woollen Mill at Kilmahog. (Craig Mair)

HAMISH

Chapter Five

Sion Barrington arrives with Hamish in 2002, the start of a whole new story. (Trossachs Woollen Mill)

Early years at Kilmahog

Hamish's move to Kilmahog was an immediate success. From the first day the staff at the Trossachs Woollen Mill loved him and he became an instant pet. He was given a paddock right next to the mill and its car park, so anyone driving past would see him, and could pull in to have a closer look.

The mill is also on a major tourist route through Scotland, on the main road from Edinburgh or Glasgow through Callander to the Trossachs or the Highlands. Buses of all sizes, carrying tourists from all countries, pass every day. Very quickly Hamish became a popular stop, where people could have a close-up experience with him, snap their photos, and take away an iconic memory of Scotland.

Of course the Trossachs Woollen Mill benefitted too. Its Scottish knitwear shop and restaurant were soon buzzing more than ever: Sion Barrington says that over the next one or two years the 'Hamish factor' added about £750,000 to the mill's profits.

The Trossachs Woollen Mill at Kilmahog, just outside Callander. (Craig Mair)

Hamish at home in his paddock at Kilmahog, and looking great. (Steven McLaren)

Hamish doing what he did best - meeting visitors. (Craig Mair)

Early years at Kilmahog

More importantly, Hamish loved the attention. When people stopped and approached his paddock he would come over to say hello and allow them to take photos. People who were his carers, and who therefore knew him especially well, remember what an instinctive poser he was - indeed, if he thought that he was not being given enough attention, he could be quite naughty. There are numerous stories of Hamish tossing someone's bag or hat into his field with a flick of his horns. Sometimes he would hook a horn into someone's sleeve to attract attention. But it was all great fun, and part of the Hamish experience.

On one occasion a young lady press photographer came with a journalist to report on the bullock at Kilmahog. Hamish decided that the lassie was not showing him enough

Oops! There goes my ring! (Jeremy Wyatt)

attention (in spite of him striking his very best poses), so with one quick twist of his enormous tongue he deftly licked the photographer's wedding ring off and swallowed it! In spite of checking Hamish's poo for some time afterwards, the ring was never recovered and it was perhaps still inside him when he died years later.

Unfortunately visitors also began to feed him whatever they had to hand. This was more worrying because Hamish would happily eat anything, even if it was not good for him. Indeed, the Herald newspaper carried an article on this by Cameron Simpson on 24th December 2002, under the heading, **Hamish must steer clear of sweets and cakes he loved**: "T'is the season to be jolly unless, that is, you are Hamish, the Highland steer. Hamish, who

Me feeding Hamish in 2007. (Craig Mair)

Early years at Kilmahog

Craig with a slice of potato for Hamish, 2010. (Craig Mair)

lives in a field next to the Trossachs Woollen Mill in Callander, Perthshire, has been put on a diet for Christmas after being stuffed like a turkey by visitors.

Sarah Winstone, a mill sales assistant, said he had been treated to an eclectic menu, from sweets and cherry scones to soup and vegetables. She said: "He will eat anything. But strawberries are one of his favourites. He gobbles most food down right away, but he likes to eat his strawberries one at a time and then lick his lips and savour the flavour …""

Thereafter, the mill shop began to provide bags of suitable food for Hamish, which visitors could then hand-feed to the gentle giant. This was normally a mixture of chopped-up turnips, potatoes, carrots, parsnips and apples.

From 2002 onwards, Hamish lived almost continuously at Kilmahog, but he still found time to make appearances elsewhere too. During the Christmas season of 2002, for example, Hamish attended the Marches shopping centre in Stirling, where he was a 'helper' at Santa's grotto. This began on 22nd November when, giving Rudolph a day off, he pulled Santa in his sleigh to the shopping centre. Next day Hamish was back on duty at Kilmahog when Santa also made a visit there to meet local boys and girls.

In 2003 John Moffat joined the staff at the mill and soon became Hamish's special carer. In those early days at Kilmahog he was able to source some food from the restaurant at Dobbie's Garden Centre in Stirling, about 15 miles away. Each night John would collect whatever unused fruit and vegetables Dobbie's had, and either feed it to Hamish or chop it up into bags for visitors to feed to him. This system worked well for a time, but eventually it ended when Dobbie's began to worry that their unused food might be re-sold elsewhere.

John had to find another source of food, so he turned to the local Co-operative shop. Hamish even had his own 'Co-op' number, and received his Co-op dividend each year! But at least John knew that when people were feeding Hamish with the centre's bags of fruit and

To begin with there was only a small fence between Hamish and his visitors. He could lean over to say hello.
(Trossachs Woollen Mill)

By about 2007 the fence had grown higher.
(Craig Mair)

If there was no-one around to brush his coat, Hamish would relieve itches by rubbing against this sign - note the bent corners! (Craig Mair)

vegetables, the bullock was eating sensible, healthy food. And of course visitors loved the close-up connection to Hamish when they fed him, even if it was across a wire fence.

One year an overseas tourist couple reversed their car up to Hamish's gate and proceeded to have a picnic at the back of their vehicle. Hamish sensed the food and immediately came over to stare and pester them into giving him some. Poor Hamish must have been tormented, but when mill manager Claire Muir pointed this out, the visitors obliged and finished their meal inside their car.

As a result of being fed all day long, Hamish also continued to grow taller and bigger. Eventually he reached a weight of approximately ¾ tonne (to know this, John Moffat had to take him to a vehicle weigh-bridge to be weighed!). In spite of this, he was always very dainty and light on his feet: Sion Barrington once told me that Highland cattle were ideal for grazing on environmentally sensitive areas where, even if they stood on rare plants such as orchids, the flowers would not be destroyed (as would have happened if any other breed of cattle had stood on them).

Hamish's horns also continued to grow. When he was just three years old at the Smith, they already had a span of 84cm but as he grew older at Kilmahog they reached a span of over one metre. People could tell his age by counting the rings on his horns (like the rings in a tree - in the case of Highland cattle, the rings are round the outside of the horns and it's one ring for each year, plus three, to give the total age). So in February 2003 Hamish would have been ten years old.

Hamish especially loved to have his coat brushed. This was usually John Moffat's job, but the mill's manageress Linda Hannah also had a party-piece for the tourists to enjoy. She would groom Hamish in the paddock for people to watch, but instead of working her way round the bullock, she would stand still and he would gradually move round her until all parts had been brushed!

By now Hamish had gained friends and admirers all over the world. People who had stopped out of curiosity at the sight of this friendly-looking bullock at the roadside, ended up keeping in touch with him for ever after. Some people made annual visits to see him. One man from Ireland came every year with a different grandchild each time. Wendy from Birmingham sent Hamish cards and money every birthday and Christmas, and also managed to visit on a bus tour most summers. Richard from Cumbernauld came regularly for years to brush Hamish's shaggy coat, even in winter. Annette Brown from Strathyre was given some of Hamish's combed-out hair, which she made into a bag for display in the handcraft section of the prestigious Royal Highland Show in Edinburgh. It won a prize in the 'something made out of an unusual fibre' category.

It is extraordinary how this bullock, plucked by chance out of obscurity at a Stirling

Early years at Kilmahog

Gerda Krijgsman from Netherlands. (Craig Mair)

Chiara Giovenzana from Italy. (George Mair)

Irene Plaza from Poland.
(Irene Plaza via Timberbush Tours)

Laury Leeds from USA.
(Laury Leeds via Timberbush Tours)

Hamish especially had female admirers all over the world!

The Peter Vardy 'Hamish' Mini. (Peter Doe, Edinburgh)

cattle market by Sion Barrington, given publicity by the chance of an art exhibition at the Smith, and rescued from BSE hysteria by a public campaign, went on to become such a part of so many people's lives for years thereafter.

When meeting Hamish, most visitors were respectful and sensible, but occasionally someone irritated him. Some people especially wanted to touch his horns, but Hamish was very choosy about who could do this. One American tourist from Texas was repeatedly advised not to touch, but he did. So with one of his special head flicks Hamish clattered him so hard that the visitor threatened to sue the mill company. Fortunately there were many witnesses to the warnings which he had been given, and in the end the gentleman accepted his fault.

By now, of course, the mill at Kilmahog was doing very well out of Hamish's popularity. Even the mill's cafe was now re-branded as 'Hamish's Coffee Shop'. By making him so freely accessible to the passing public, he had become a star attraction, an iconic subject for

Early years at Kilmahog

photographers and artists. The internet is full of images of Hamish taken by people from all over the world. Of course Hamish loved the attention, and seemed to specially pose, just for you. People loved it. As American blogger Kate Cowie Riley wrote online in November 2014, "He was there to greet the thousands of visitors who stopped at the Mill on their way through the Trossachs. Hamish continued to pose for many artists, one dubbed him the Kate Moss of the Highland Coo world because he looked so good, even on bad hair days."

Eventually someone began to produce Hamish memorabilia. This was not really the kind of merchandise appropriate to the Smith Art Gallery and Museum in Stirling, but before long the Trossachs Woollen Mill's gift shop was well stocked with everything from post cards and fridge magnets to tea towels, drinks coasters and key rings. These sold well to Hamish's growing fan club, especially to children who could now purchase an affordable souvenir of the big hairy Scottish Coo.

Occasionally Hamish appeared on TV. One example was in 2006 when the BBC made a programme retracing the journey made by an open-topped car from Land's End in the south of England to John o' Groats in the north of Scotland in 1925, and which was filmed in colour - groundbreaking technology at that time. In the original, the motor car's occupants meet a scrawny old Highland cow at Kilmahog - but in the BBC's re-enactment they meet Hamish!

Unfortunately they decided to film after closing time at the mill. What they did not realise was that Hamish regarded this as the end of his working day too, and would go off to the furthest corner of his field for a lie down. Here he would turn his back to the car park and rest contentedly after the exertion of meeting fans all day. It took much rattling of cattle food dishes to persuade him to come back for the TV cameras.

On another occasion the Peter Vardy car dealership launched a new promotional campaign round a Highland bull called Hamish. This featured a Mini car which had been crossed with a Highland bull so that it had a hairy exterior, a fine set of horns on top, a pink tongue hanging out below the front grill, a tail on the back wiper and a car horn which mooed!

HAMISH His Story

Hamish accompanies Santa on a visit to the Thistles shopping mall in Stirling. (Sion Barrington)

Christmas was a special time for Hamish. Having already helped several times to bring Santa Claus to Callander, and also to Stirling, he and Santa soon formed a strong friendship. Like everyone else, Santa quickly grew to love Hamish and soon he came up with an idea. Everyone knew that on Christmas Eve, Santa's leading reindeer Rudolph was usually very tired by the time he reached Callander, so Santa asked if Rudolph could rest for a bit at Kilmahog while Hamish took over the pulling of Santa's sleigh - after all, Hamish knew his way through the highland glens better than Rudolph and could help Santa deliver his presents much more quickly. Santa's visits became an annual Christmas tradition at Kilmahog, and Hamish was always there to greet him. Many children wrote their Christmas letters to him, to pass on to Santa when he visited. Of course Hamish also received so many Christmas cards from well-wishers across the world that he became rather envied by some of the mill staff!

During those earlier years at Kilmahog, Hamish lived in his paddock virtually all year round, in all weathers. Highland cattle are famous for their cold weather hardiness: according to Sion Barrington the Highland breed is the only breed in Scandinavia and Germany which is allowed to be left out in the fields by farmers during their cold and snowy winters. During the severe winter of 2010, however, the Callander area had such heavy falls of snow that the roof of Hamish's shelter shed collapsed - much to his dismay and disapproval.

Despite such occasional upsets, these were very happy times for Hamish. But what he did not have, however, was the company of other animals in his paddock. The staff at Kilmahog still remember how, in 2004, the local farmer put some Blackface sheep into the

February 2009 and Hamish celebrates his 17th birthday in his paddock at Kilmahog.
(Whyler Photos, Stirling)

field next to Hamish's paddock. A few of the lambs somehow managed to wriggle through the fence and came to investigate Hamish. This really frightened him, for he was not used to having other creatures in his field.

On another occasion the farmer had some Charolais cattle grazing in his field. Even though they were creamy-coloured and with no long shaggy hair or big horns, Hamish seems to have enjoyed having some similar creatures to himself as neighbours. The mill staff still remember well how miserable he was when the Charolais were eventually taken away again.

What Hamish really needed was some Highland cattle companions in his own paddock.

December 2010 and Hamish gets some hay to eat.
In the background is his shelter shed with its collapsed roof. (Steven McLaren)

HAMISH

Chapter Six

Hamish with Honey in the summer of 2011. (Steven McLaren)

New friends for Hamish

In 2010 the management at the Trossachs Woollen Mill finally decided that Hamish should have some company in his paddock. Apart from the thought that it would be nice for Hamish, there was also the concern that Hamish had already lived much longer than the average number of years for Highland bullocks - it would make sense to introduce another Highlander to the mill as a future attraction already in place when Hamish finally passed away.

And so in late April, the new cow arrived. This was Heather, another fine example of the Highland breed. Her arrival was electrifying - the mill staff can still clearly remember the excitement which Hamish showed when she first appeared out of her trailer and nosed her way into the paddock. They say that he was almost dancing with pleasure.

Heather with Hamish. (Steven McLaren)

Claire Muir, then the manageress at the mill, said in a press interview at the time, "Hamish has always been happy, but we decided to bring in a female from a breeder in Fife to keep him company. As soon as the trailer backed into the field and she trotted in, he did a Highland Fling. It was hilarious. He was prancing around to impress her and, though she wasn't sure about him at first, they have settled down very happily together. They lie down together and she scratches his belly with her horns. They even kiss".

Of course the arrival of female company was very quickly described by the Scottish media as a romance. In spite of the fact that Hamish was a bullock (and not a bull), this inconvenient point was not allowed to get in the way of a good story, as in this extract from a lighthearted piece on STV's news broadcast on 28th May 2010: "A story set in the Scottish countryside has seen two lovers conquer the odds against them. He's been a bachelor all his days and she is 13 years younger, but in Callander's own version of 'May to September', Hamish

This was the kind of 'will she, won't she?' picture which the press loved. (Craig Mair)

New friends for Hamish

Heather learned from Hamish and became another big attraction for visitors. (Craig Mair)

and Heather have fallen in love. Hamish - who just happens to be a Highland bull - has been a bachelor for years. He is a star attraction at the Trossachs Woollen Mill in Kilmahog, near Callander. He has never been lonely, with lots of visitors. But Hamish had never had a female companion until now.

Lesley O'Neill from the Trossachs Woollen Mill said: "They fell in love at first sight, and Hamish was actually doing the Highland Fling. All of a sudden he's become ten years younger." Hamish became famous when he was saved from the slaughterhouse at the height of the BSE crisis. Now an ageing bull at 17, the staff here wanted him to have a mate. It's easy to see why Heather fell for Hamish. He's eligi-bull, relia-bull, adora-bull, and lova-bull! ... Lesley said: "Heather keeps him in his place, and it's obvious who wears the trousers. Like any other relationship they have their ups and downs, but it's fantastic ...""

Soon well-wishing cards, gifts and Valentines began to arrive at Kilmahog from people all over the world as, even in far away Australia, people felt delight for Hamish. To add a bit more spice to the story, the mill staff even held a fun wedding ceremony for the two animals!

HAMISH His Story

Honey, just three months old in June 2011. (Trossachs Woollen Mill)

For a time Hamish truly enjoyed the companionship of Heather. As visitor numbers increased with the onset of the tourist season, they were usually seen standing or lying close to each other in their field. Eventually, however, Heather became too boisterous and dominant for Hamish's liking. I feel that he had grown up with no herd experience and perhaps, as a life-long bachelor, he had simply become too set in his ways.

Two of Hamish's greatest fans were Nancy and her mother Isa, who lived in Kilsyth, about 30 miles away. For ten years these two ladies came every single day to visit Hamish and to bring him some food - always the very best, bought at the up-market Marks and Spencers store. Indeed, the mill shop would temporarily stop providing visitors with its own bags of cattle food while the two ladies were there with Hamish. However, now that Heather had arrived, Nancy and Isa began to find that she would not let Hamish share their food and, in the end, they had to devise a way to feed them separately. But they always made sure that Hamish got all the carrots!

New friends for Hamish

In an attempt to give Hamish some respite from Heather, the mill staff put up an electric fence between them, but even this made no difference. Perhaps the voltage was too low, or possibly Heather's shaggy coat acted as an insulator, but she often just pushed the electric wire down and came through to pester Hamish.

In June 2011 the Trossachs Woollen Mill acquired another new arrival for Hamish. This was a beautiful young calf called Honey, which had been born in March that year. Of course the press could not resist the temptation to describe Honey as the result of the 'romance' between Hamish and Heather. In this, they were admittedly aided and abetted by the mill staff, for even manageress Claire Muir was quoted as having said, "We are thrilled that

The Trossachs Woollen Mill held a competition to guess the name of the new arrival. Claire Muir, manager (centre) with 1st prize winner Lynne Hope and 2nd prize winners. (Whyler Photos)

Hamish and Heather now have a gorgeous baby calf, and we know our visitors will absolutely love her". Strictly speaking this was true, even if mischievously misleading, but soon the newspapers were full of stories about 'Hamish the Highland bull, Heather the heifer and her calf', or how 'Hamish the Highland bull has become a father for the first time' (which, as the Smith's website later pointed out, was "no mean feat for a bullock!").

Whatever the spin given to the arrival of Honey, she turned out to be very popular, both with Hamish and the public. Having allowed the press time to play with the idea of

In March 2012 Hamish and Honey shared a birthday cake.
Manageress Claire Muir is seen here posing for the press. (Whyler Photos, Stirling)

May 2012 and Hamish is still wowing the visitors. (Craig Mair)

'Hamish, his wife Heather and their calf Honey', Heather was eventually transferred to a new home at the Loch Achray Hotel, a few miles away in the Trossachs, where she became a great attraction for visitors there.

For a time Hamish happily shared his paddock with just Honey. This time he was the boss! In September 2013 Clogblog from Holland posted online a typical example of the visitor experience: "Hamish has to be the most well-known and most visited Highland cow in Scotland. Many tourist buses stop here daily for admirers of this coo. Hamish is incredibly friendly and gentle despite his size, and loves having his picture taken. We bought a pack of Hamish approved food from the mill shop and enjoyed feeding him his vegetables. His tongue is huge but he takes each piece so gently. It was really fun. He was quite greedy and even pushed Honey out of the way for more snacks and photos!"

By this time John Moffat was sourcing much of his cattle feed from the Boquhan Estate near Kippen, from where the superb farm shop run by Jim and Robbie McKechnie delivered supplies to Kilmahog every day. Hamish and Honey might not have known it, but they were eating the finest Scottish produce.

By now the Trossachs Woollen Mill had become a top attraction for tour buses. Rabbie's Trail Burners, Timberbush Tours and others all saw Hamish at Kilmahog as an essential stop for their passengers and even had posters of him in their booking offices. Edinburgh tour operator Donald Finlayson became a fan and such a regular visitor that he even founded 'The Hairy Coo' bus tour company to share his passion for Hamish with everyone else.

Donald told me: "Our domain name and our trading name was actually inspired by Hamish himself. In 2005, I was trying to develop various ideas for a coach tour company and came up with the idea of orange or ginger coaches that looked like 'hairy coos'. Hairy Coo was my pet name for these wonderful creatures when I was a lad. It was whilst looking through some old photos that I found one of Hamish and the thought crossed my mind that he was in fact 'The Hairy Coo' rather than just any Hairy Coo. I went online, bought the domain name and 4 years later ... turned the idea into a reality. So Hamish was, and always shall be, 'The Hairy Coo'".

Blogger Roddy MacLeod from the USA posted in 2012 how he'd: "noticed what a fantastic attraction Hamish is for the tourists. Many touring bus trips stop at the retail outlet and the tourists actually run over from their buses to take photos of Hamish. They also buy vegetable blocks from the shop so that they can feed him, and they get quite excited about seeing highland cattle. Hamish does very well, and so does the Mill shop. These sorts of things are exactly what tourists, and children, like to see, and there's nothing wrong with that at all. It's part of the Scottish heritage."

By now Hamish was getting on in years. Each year the mill staff at Kilmahog lovingly made a birthday cake for him, although in 2012 he shared it with Honey whose birthday was

New friends for Hamish

Hamish, Hamish Dubh and Honey looking up from their feeding trough when we arrived for a visit.

Hamish was delighted to see John and came over immediately to greet us.

Hamish still loved to be stroked and scratched.

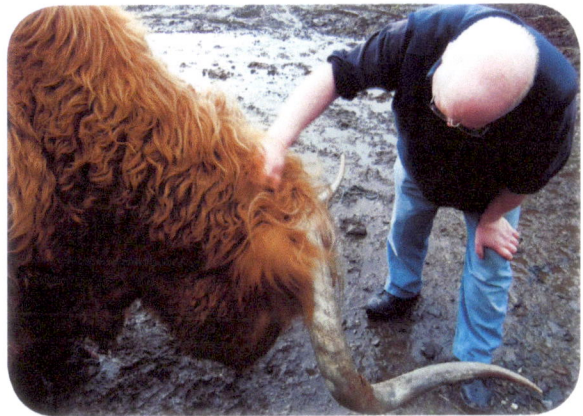

John Moffat, his carer, shared a great bond with Hamish and could stand much closer to his horns than I might do.

John Moffat and I visiting Hamish at his winter farm accommodation in January 2013. (Craig Mair)

Hamish heading the new 'family' of Honey and Hamish Dubh. (Steven McLaren)

in early March. It was a photo opportunity not missed by the press and those hardier tourists out and about in a Scottish winter. Birthday cards also arrived from far and wide, many from abroad.

Then in June 2012 Hamish Dubh arrived. He was a fine young black bullock calf - dubh (pronounced like 'doo') is Gaelic for black. He made an excellent companion for Hamish and Honey and quickly attracted lots of interest. At a press gathering to announce Hamish Dubh's arrival, Claire Muir, the general manager of the Trossachs Woollen Mill said, "We are all very excited about the calf. I am sure visitors during the summer will be thrilled to see the new addition to Hamish's family and hope that lots of local people will come along to see our new arrival too."

To celebrate Hamish Dubh's arrival, the woollen mill also held another competition to guess the newcomer's birthday. The prize was a 'Highland Coo Hamper' from the mill shop. This new bullock was an excellent addition to the paddock. Being black, he was a bit different from the normal tan colour of Highland cattle.

Being still a calf he was cute, like Honey. And of course he 'knew his place' and dutifully gave way to the old master when required - at mealtimes there was still very much a pecking order, and Hamish always went first!

Hamish's 20th birthday in 2013, and he's making sure that he gets the cake before the younger ones!
(Whyler Photos, Stirling)

By now Hamish was being sent to a local farm during the coldest winter months, with Honey and Hamish Dubh also for company. No-one was very sure if such an old Highlander would still be able to withstand Scotland's cold winter rain, sleet and snow, so at Robert Scott's farm he had shelter and straw, and knowledgeable people to watch over him.

Recently vet Ian Rodger emailed me to say: "Most of the time this arrangement worked well, however in the summer of 2012, which was exceptionally wet, we noted he was losing condition. A clinical examination and blood and dung tests showed that liver fluke was indeed a problem, and he was moved for the rest of the year back to the farm, to drier pasture and preferential feeding in a farm shed, keeping the weather off his back. This allowed him to regain condition. The fluke parasite thrives in wet conditions as part of it's life cycle involves a mud snail, which was found almost everywhere that year. Thankfully he recovered, and was back the following year, at the woollen mill".

As soon as the worst of each winter was over, he would be returned to his paddock and back to his admiring visitors. Indeed, his carer John Moffat says that when Hamish realised that he was about to be moved from the farm back to Kilmahog, he would come "skipping out of his shed like a spring lamb".

HAMISH

Chapter Seven

Hamish (Trossachs Woollen Mill)

Hamish in old age

In February 2013 Hamish reached his 20th birthday. He was getting old - most bullocks which are allowed to live beyond an early slaughter don't exceed fourteen years. Mill manageress Clair Muir began to make enquiries about having Hamish assessed by the Guinness Book of Records as possibly the oldest living bullock in the world. The records people were genuinely interested but it was discovered that Hamish was not the world's oldest living bullock, as there was an older one somewhere in India (where cattle are protected and are not allowed to be killed). However, there was a strong chance that he was the oldest anywhere outside India. We may never know for sure, but Hamish was often described as the oldest bullock in Britain, which was almost certainly true.

In February 2013 Hamish's birthday cake was presented to him in a field with snow all around. It was difficult to judge when conditions were good enough to return him from his winter farm accommodation to the Woollen Mill, and sometimes the three cattle would be caught out by a later fall of snow. But it didn't seem to trouble them much, and the snow rarely lay for long.

As the years passed at Kilmahog, Hamish was obviously beginning to feel his age. In particular, he was such a big heavy boy that his legs and feet began to suffer. Like many humans he also began to develop arthritis in his hips and lower back. On at least one occasion he contracted pneumonia - it was a very good summer and the staff thought that he was suffering from heat, but the vet diagnosed pneumonia and gave him antibiotics.

Hamish's vets were Struthers and Scott at nearby Doune, a well-respected and popular veterinary practice. In the early days John Struthers himself tended to Hamish, and occasionally had to treat his ailments. Later the practice joined forces with the Grahams Road Veterinary Clinic in Falkirk for the specialist care of farm animals and horses. Under the new name of Forth Valley Vets they now worked from a base in Stirling. While Struthers and Scott continued with the treatment of small animals at their practice in Doune, Hamish's care was now taken on by this group of farm animal vets, including Ian Rodger, Paddy Day, Alisdair Smith and others.

Following the BSE outbreak in the summer of 1996 Hamish's cattle passport (which all cattle in the UK must have) was marked 'Not for Human Consumption', meaning that he could never enter the food chain. This allowed the vets to prescribe oral painkillers for Hamish's arthritis - anti-inflammatories for horses and normally not used for cattle. Ian Rodger remembers one occasion when, at a routine visit to assess if Hamish was well enough to be

Honey, photographed on 30th April 2014 and now a lot bigger than the cute baby calf which had arrived at Kilmahog in 2012. (Trossachs Woollen Mill)

Hamish Dubh, photographed on 6th April 2014 and already considerably bigger than Honey. By now he was developing into an impressive big beast, as Hamish, seen here in the background, struggled with old age. (David Kerr Gray)

given more medication, the staff could not catch the old boy, which prompted vet Alisdair Smith to comment, "Well the painkillers must be working then!"

In his old age Hamish also increasingly came to have trouble with his feet. The section of his paddock closest to the car park, where Hamish posed mostly for visitors, would become very muddy and churned up - so much so that the mill staff eventually had a concrete area laid there in 2011. Nevertheless, Hamish sometimes had foot rot in his aging feet. With such tender hooves, standing on any hard stone would cause him to limp, while any cut would allow infections to get into his feet.

Hamish in July 2014, too tired to get up and greet his visitors (Graeme Mair)

To treat this problem a machine was needed to keep Hamish still, but also to make his feet accessible to the vets. A special contraption like a cattle crush was used - this was like a cage with strong railings which could be closed tighter once Hamish was inside - this was done hydraulically by power from a tractor. It was expensive to hire and had to be brought many miles from a farm in the Scottish borders, so it was used only when it was really necessary.

Once Hamish had been pushed into this cage and his horns had been carefully adjusted round the rails, a strap was passed under his belly and tightened to hold him in place. The crush was then swung over so that Hamish was tipped onto his side, which gave easy access to any feet needing attention. It was quite a sight to see this cage with Hamish encased in it and lying on his side - it was certainly undignified for the poor old boy and he really hated it, but it was for his own good. Any problem could then be treated without the vet being kicked, and Hamish could even be given a full foot pedicure before being tipped upright again and released from his confinement.

On at least one occasion Hamish had a really painful foot abscess. This required a special hot poultice to treat it. However the muddy ground shrank the cloth used to apply the dressing so that it twisted tighter into his hoof. In the end Hamish had to be tied to a fence post while the cloth was cut off. It's not easy to lift the leg of a ¾ tonne bullock, but he stood perfectly still while the sole of his foot was pared to allow the pus to drain out.

One of the last photos of Hamish, taken in October 2014 by Brandy Sinisi of Connecticut, USA.
He looks tired and boney, and old.

HAMISH His Story

All his life Hamish loved his vegetables, but in 2013 the staff at Kilmahog began to realise that he was losing weight, and that he was dropping a lot of his food (much to the delight of Hamish Dubh and Honey!). This was a big problem, for without an adequate diet Hamish would just fade away to skin and bone. More veterinary advice was sought and it was soon found that, after so many years of use, Hamish's teeth had worn away. He could no longer chew or break up his favourite (but crunchy) potatoes, carrots and turnips. Since there was no way of sharpening what remained of his teeth, Hamish was put onto a diet of what was basically baby food, or calf cake. This was a mixture of coarse flakes, food pellets high in protein and energy, and chopped-up alpha grass (since he could no longer eat hay).

In July 2014 the Commonwealth Games were held in Glasgow. Prior to this the Queen's Baton was carried by runners across Commonwealth nations throughout the world. On its return to Scotland, it was taken by baton bearers to communities all over Scotland. Here the staff of the Trossachs Woollen Mill proudly hold the baton during its journey in the Trossachs (Steven McLaren)

Meanwhile, the food provided in bags for the tourists to use was also chopped up into much smaller pieces than before.

All this makes Hamish sound sad and pathetic in his old age, but this was far from true. Indeed, from January 2012 he had his own Facebook page - his first post was, **Thinking of having some grass**, which was a perfectly bullock-like thing to say. On the other hand, in May 2012 he posted, "First time I had chocolate today, tasted amazing at first, however I've got a very sore stomach now :(". This attracted 43 get-well-soon messages (and a few more from people offering to eat the chocolate for him).

Hamish also liked to remind people to pay him enough attention, especially since he now had younger competition. Even at his winter hideaway, if farmer Robert Scott didn't bring his feed soon enough he was likely to be butted into the water trough. His carer John Moffat also remembers a few similar 'reminders' from old Hamish. More than once John or assistant Georgie went into his paddock with buckets of food, but had to nip smartly back over the gate again as Hamish chased them for being so late. He certainly had not lost his spark!

On 31st July 2013 a helicopter landed right beside Hamish, much to his great interest. At about lunchtime that day an 82 year old, but heavy, gentleman suffered cardiac arrest on a tour bus which had just arrived at the mill. Unfortunately he was at the back of the bus and it required an experienced first response team to get him out and make him ready for the ambulance which had also been called. Having diagnosed cardiac arrest, an air ambulance was scrambled and soon arrived overhead. Part of the mill's car park was therefore cleared of vehicles to create a landing area.

Meanwhile, in spite of desperate attempts to resuscitate the patient he passed away, and was therefore taken in the ambulance to the Royal Forth Valley hospital. This meant that the Helimed 5 helicopter (EC-135 G-SASA) would not be required and could return to its Glasgow base, so with a great roar of engines it fired up again to take off. The noise might have frightened many animals, but not Hamish - indeed, he came over to his fence, to be nearer

I'm standing beside the big Hamish sign at Kilmahog,
where people had already attached a wreath and a bunch of flowers. (Craig Mair)

Hamish in old age

while he watched with much interest as the helicopter rose and flew away.

As a sad footnote to this, it should be mentioned that the pilot on that day was David Traill. In November 2013 he was flying a police helicopter when it suffered double engine failure and crashed into the roof of the Clutha Vaults bar in Glasgow. He was one of ten people killed in that dreadful incident.

From even his earliest days at the Smith Art Gallery and Museum, Hamish loved to be groomed. Over the years many people, especially children and those with special needs, had the privilege of doing this and he loved it. But as he grew older Hamish's magnificent body began to get thinner. He was shrinking with age and no longer relished being groomed so much, especially when he had more tangles in his coat. Previously they would have been no problem to groom out, but as time passed the tugging and pulling become too much for Hamish. Like any ageing body, he just preferred to be left alone.

By the summer of 2014 Honey and Hamish Dubh had been companions in the same paddock with old Hamish for a couple of years, and were beginning to develop their own individual personalities. Although the two young ones were only a few months different in age, Hamish Dubh was now growing much bigger than Honey. He was also developing the steadier personality, learning from old Hamish how to play to the crowd and how to pose for photos. The young bullock's horns were also growing bigger - but sideways, with no great signs of Hamish's famous upward curve. That may yet happen with time, but by later 2014 Hamish Dubh was already shaping up into a magnificent big beast. Honey had meanwhile become more mischievous and unpredictable, quite a lot smaller than Hamish Dubh but a lot of fun for visitors.

In November 2014 Hamish, Hamish Dubh and Honey were taken off to their farmyard winter quarters as usual each year. Here they had good overnight and day cover from the weather and beds of straw to lie on. As a standard precaution the vet attended and took some blood samples, but the results were good. There was nothing to worry about.

Two of the wreaths received at the mill on display in the shop. Part of the card reads
"Thank you Hamish for the love, joy, warmth, friendship and laughter you brought into our lives."
(Angela Stewart Mair)

It was on this comfortable bed, surrounded by his 'family', that Hamish passed away quietly in his sleep on Monday 3rd November. He was 21 years and 9 months old. There is a tear in my eye as I write this, because it was the end of an era. When mill staff went to visit Hamish next morning they found him lying on the ground as if he was sleeping, but as Claire Muir said, "While it was very sad, it was the best way for him to go. We knew he had been fine right up to the last and when the time came he went suddenly". Or as vet Ian Rodger said recently, "Hamish lived a trouble-free and long life", and I suppose that is all any of us could ever hope for.

News of Hamish's death spread quickly, first to the local and national Scottish newspapers, but then all round the world. Mill manageress Claire Muir said to the press: "… We all have great memories of him. The minute I spoke outside he would turn his head. He had an amazing and healthy life … We have all been a bit upset and teary. We have had customers tearful when they found out as well, and many people came once or twice a week to see him. But he lived way beyond what anyone would expect and we have to be content with the fact he had a happy life. He was so placid for his size and ability, very gentle …"

At the Smith Art Gallery and Museum in Stirling, curator Elspeth King said, "Having learned of the death of our magnificent 'publicity coo' there wasn't a dry eye in the Smith. It is a sad day for all of us in the Smith".

Very soon Hamish's Facebook page and lots of Twitter accounts began to carry messages of sadness and condolences. RIP messages came from as far afield as Wrexham in Wales, Calcutta in India and Newcastle in New South Wales, Australia. Emails, cards and flowers also started to arrive at the mill.

One typical email came from Heidi Bryner, a teacher in a small town in Pennsylvania, USA, who wrote: "I brought a group of 50 high school students and parents to Scotland this past June and we were lucky to have met Hamish while on tour. He was so kind, gentle and beautiful. He was one of our highlights of Scotland. The kids thought he was so 'cool'! We are just getting the news about his passing and we would like to extend our deepest sympathies to you and your families because we know how much Hamish meant to you. We will send lots of prayers your way and tell stories about the day we met Hamish to keep his memory alive".

Another came from Stefan Heck in Germany, who said simply, "I am very sorry to read that Hamish is not more beside us. I visited him twice on our holidays this year and two years before".

I think it may be the same Stef who also blogged on December 5th: "I have quite the lump in my throat and don't know how to start this post. I was looking forward to telling you all about Hamish and to tell you to make sure you go visit him too. That's history now. I still want to write about our visit and at least tell you what a great gentle giant he was. Although it's sad, that you won't get to visit him anymore, at least you'll have heard of his story ... better than nothing ... and I thoroughly believe the best way to honor someone, no matter if human or cherished animal, is to keep the memory alive. Hamish - you were loved by fans all over the world and will always be remembered!"

It is extraordinary how Hamish's death touched so many people, all around the world.

Hamish will be a hard act to follow. He had become Callander's own Braveheart, Stirlingshire's favourite, always-hungry, big Hairy Coo. A Scottish icon loved across the world. Now younger cattle must replace the old boy at Kilmahog - and they undoubtedly will. In December 2014 Claire Muir said: "Honey and Hamish Dubh have spent the past couple of years learning their picture posing from the great master. We hope that our valued customers and visitors will continue to show their affection for our two beautiful Highland cattle, and ensure they are loved in the way Hamish was for so many years".

Hamish and I knew each other for nearly 20 years. I will miss him terribly, but so will many others all over the world, for he inspired us, made us care for him, gave us fun, joy, and finally sadness. He may have been just a hairy old coo who could never have known the emotions he aroused in others, but he will surely be remembered fondly as a true Scottish legend for many, many years to come.

Hamish (Craig Mair)

www.ingramcontent.com/pod-product-compliance
Lightning Source LLC
Chambersburg PA
CBHW042034150426
43201CB00002B/18